How To Know You're Dreaming When You're Dreaming, Lesson One

Angelica Maria Barraza Tran

AN INLANDIA INSTITUTE PUBLICATION

RIVERSIDE, CALIFORNIA

Library of Congress Cataloging-in-Publication Data

Names: Barraza Tran, Angelica Maria, author.
Title: How to know you're dreaming when you're dreaming, lesson one / Angelica Maria Barraza Tran.
Other titles: How to know you're dreaming when you're dreaming, lesson 1
Description: First edition. | Riverside, California : Inlandia Institute, [2023]
Identifiers: LCCN 2023003977 | ISBN 9781955969147 (paperback)
Subjects: LCSH: Latin Americans--Poetry. | Latin America--Poetry. | LCGFT: Poetry. | Creative nonfiction.
Classification: LCC PS3602.A777464 H69 2023 | DDC 811/.6--dc23/eng/20230206
LC record available at https://lccn.loc.gov/2023003977

Published by Inlandia Institute
Riverside, California
www.InlandiaInstitute.org
First Edition

*How To Know You're Dreaming
When You're Dreaming, Lesson One*

Angelica Maria Barraza Tran

for Marc

acknowledgments:

"Still Life with Mexico" first appeared in *The Journal of Latina Critical Feminism*; "For You, Malinalli" in *Southern Humanities Review*; "Seven Ways of Looking at Tayeko's Hands" in *Cipactli*, "Summoning Quetzals" in *"re-knewing"* by *apo-press

DREAMS THAT ARE NOT

DREAMS TOUCHING WATER

GLOSSARY OF COMMON SYMBOLS

DREAMS THAT ARE NOT

There's a dream I have in which I love the world. I run from
end to end like fingers through her hair. There are no borders,
only wind. Like you, I was born. Like you, I was raised in
the institution of dreaming. Hand on my heart. Hand on my
stupid heart.

Cameron Awkward Rich

STILL LIFE WITH MEXICO

1

His parents left him in this country when he was nine. He didn't want to stay but his father insisted, likening him to a tree. When it's small, he said, you prop it up with sticks. But then it grows and gets big and you take the sticks away.

I don't think he ever recovered, my father. His branches never swelled with fruit. The bark of his trunk shed in excess from his body, littering the floor of so many government apartments. I don't think his parents had a choice. But also maybe they did. They kissed his forehead and got in the car, crossing the border back into Mexico.

2

In so many dreams I have adopted his perspective at the moment of abandonment. I have stood for so long in the same place that when I moved my knees buckled; I have wept to the sputtering of exhaust, searched the clouds for a familiar shape before the wind teased it away.

In my dreams I look down at my boy body, take inventory of my boy fingers and shins. Note how the summer asphalt breaches the soles of my sandals, holding me in its wild heat.

3

Growing up all I knew of Mexico was the way my father looked at things for long stretches of time without actually seeing them. He took to drinking with the midnight fervor of an artist, only he never made anything beautiful. I used to lay awake in bed at night waiting for the sound of his boots coming up the stairs, for the whistle on his lips and the salt on his breath. Other times I lay awake wishing he would run after the car. Twenty years later I wanted him to chase it down, beg his parents to keep him, to prop him up just a little longer that he might one day touch god's chin.

4

When my grandpa died, my father's father, there was a seven-day funeral in the town of Talpa de Allende in his honor. My father went alone while my mother stayed back in the states to look after my sister and I. We watched syndicated episodes of Lois and Clark. We listened to the radio and ate cereal dry. We almost missed him, or we missed him horribly. The shadow of my father's ghost thinned, then disappeared from our home altogether.

On the sixth night the phone rang. It was a collect call. My mother accepted, held the receiver to her ear and nodded. Then nodded again. She returned to the dinner table and didn't say a word.

Driving to the airport several days later her knuckles turned white where they gripped the wheel. She looked at my sister and I with the corners of her eyes. She said she had something to tell us.

It's your father, she said. There's been an accident. He was breaking a horse on the ranch but instead the horse broke him. It bucked him off, and before he could get away a hoof, with incredible force, made contact with his head. She said, We don't know how long it's going to last. She said, He doesn't remember us. He doesn't remember a thing.

My sister heaved beside me. The freeway suddenly felt like the saddest place in the world. How many times had I darkly wished that something like this would happen.

That some abominable miracle would touch our family, pull us dripping from the river of Lethe. I felt like all my wanting had conspired to nurture the horse's disobedience. But I also felt like the horse had given him something, given *us* something, through the mercy of forgetting.

5

Just after my 26th birthday my father asked me to go to Mexico with him. I had been before, on short trips to Baja, but never to the place of his childhood. I didn't know what to bring, or how to prepare myself to arrive somewhere I had for so long imagined as a distant, far away place.

We boarded a flight from LAX to Puerto Vallarta. A man awaited us holding a cardboard sign with our last name scrawled across it. He took us in his truck outside the city, down dirt roads lined with narrow trees, through plazas, across narrow bridges flanked on both sides by blue agave fields. I knew we made it when my father rolled down his window and began greeting the people we passed, tilting his hat to their tilted hats. We pulled up a long driveway to a wooden house situated in the middle of a sprawling ranch, dotted with horses, cattle, chickens and pigs. I got out of the truck and stretched my legs. A string of people lined up to kiss our cheeks.

Over the next week my father and I loosened into the daily rhythms of a lost life. At sunrise we woke to milk the cows while their calves impatiently looked on from the other side of the fence. During the day I'd walk the oxbow ravine, or squat beside the river, proselytizing to the reeds. At night we'd sit around the porch in mismatched plastic chairs. I eluded questions about boyfriends to the compositions of cricket song. Encased between two cousins, sleep coaxed me. I stirred only briefly at the weight of a beetle as it landed on my throat.

Why did he never move back? Why did he choose to remain in the states, even after he was old enough to make the return journey on his own? I asked as he leaned against a dead tree, chewing a toothpick to splinters. He said, this isn't my home anymore. And if I moved back, I'd probably just drink myself to death.

I leaned against the same tree and looked out over the ranch. I tried to see it as he did. I tried to feel the wind, the way it howled against his face. But I couldn't. My father walked back up the drive into the house, and I realized the longing was mine. It was me who saw Mexico in everything. In the oblong shadows my body cast across the dirt; in the ceiling of my bedroom, gazing down upon me as I dreamed with open eyes.

For You, Malinalli

Show me how to conjure an axe to sever
the nautilus of a 500-year-old ship. I will swing it
wild, like it was born of my own pleasure-seeking flesh,
the blade a bone organizing the tilt of my pelvis,
a bleached white key to my architectural
center. Pick me up in a pulse of sinew and light.
Manipulate skillfully the elemental forces, wager
everything on a caress. I spill out onto the deck of pale faced
men drenching their boots in the impossible.
Historical erasure begins in the mouth. I loll my tongue
in invocation: an anti-prayer to the tides, beseeching them to carry
progress backward to the old world.

Unname hispana, untouch communal sands.
If I can create life I can restore the logic of the gift—

Elegy for a Portrait Artist

Then her body peeled
away like husk;
    beneath
smooth river stone,
chiseled by moon's corner.

Rogue artist

        of the garden—

Her portrait will be too heavy
to hang, rendered with paints
inexact in their
        coloring;
her jaw an abstract shape
from which critics will locate
impressions of hunger.

Deer mother,
mother of hummingbird
song, I would've pulled
your remains from the oven if
        I understood:

in life, your body was never
        your own.

I would've dipped you
        breathless
into fragrant creek water,
washed you of your husband's
name, dressed you
in finery, threaded ivy
through thin curls.

I would've placed poetry
        on your searching
tongue before laying you free
to reign in the kingdom
of dirt.

In Response to Swampbody

for Ana Mendieta

Drag out back door down tall grass lined with taller grass. Drag easel. Drag brush. Line each pigment on a warm rock by the water—colors you know she is. A few she isn't, or just hasn't been yet. Adjust yourself until the angle is exactly where she wants you. Create borders inside the canvas with tape. Anticipate paint bleed. Make a show of containment.

(Don't mind that she hasn't let you see her in weeks. Don't mind her handprint shallowing on surfaces you thought permanent. Or that you were never the artist she spoke of you being.)

Ana emerges from blackwater swampbody. Algae cling algae drip. Wading through swampwater towards you : her blackbody, your blackbodies. The hues are not dark enough to capture. She comes slowly, black hair sticking to swampbone, crawling branches down backwater, algaehair, algaeskin tips, algaelip press. Parts of Ana dripping back into blackswamp. [Your wrist cannot move fast enough. Pieces of this will not be documented] Waterswamp waterbody. Ana emerging algaecling, dissolving in bodywater, shedding blacklayer, becoming smaller. [she is always smallest next to you]

She reaches tall grass and the canvas means nothing. SwampAna turning to grassAna, only she is still wet, she is always emerging. Algaedrip footstep trailing from waterbody, as she circles the porch circles the porch circles the porch before calling for you to follow

The American Dream Depends on Who is Dreaming

you have a very mexican vagina

> that's what he said, the first time rafa saw it

vicky just giggled, my shorts in her hand

> her shorts in her hand, my shirt in her hand

no way, loren said. actually, he kind of gasped it

> he'd never seen one before. he poked it & brought his finger
> to his nose to sniff

solmayra had said it looked like a flower

> i asked what kind & she said she didn't know. she got quiet after that

> —i'd hoped she'd say lily

tita, rest in peace, used to talk to it with her eyes

> i imagined the dialogue as her pupils shifted. something about
> los cielos

> & the opposite of god

> & Sappho's thumb

the first time i saw it i was fourteen.

> my dad came home with mirrored closet doors—

> i sat on the carpet beneath the tiny window & looped my feet
> out of jeans.

when my legs parted i understood

> the inevitable truth of flowers, the gospel of solitude
> & the ghostly shapes of immanent matter.

i too understood that one day i'd know ripe fruit by touch,
>   that i'd cut onions with dry eyes, that i would journey to
>   cross and re-cross
>   the borders of my body

I knew that truth is experiential,
>   & no knowledge is complete until I feel it,
>   here—

ENDLING

when you touch the last of its kind
remember its chosen name
use yr hands to whisper it
into fur & marrow
& when you stop it'll disappear
so don't ever stop
a touch withdrawn is an unuttered
prayer

when an era ends
—its skin falling
into grass &
lashes into
moonlit lace—

  it is time for you to gather:

braid an effigy of animal
dreams that no beast
is truly lost
that they ride eternal
the air in a flurry
of irreproducible ashes

The disaster broke before the story. Some say the story precipitated the disaster and this can be corroborated by eyewitness birds. The story is a continuation of yesterday's headline only more children are missing. The numbers of the deceased multiplied by the millions of individual grains of Saharan dust circulating the globe. The dirt kicked up by an impromptu conga line could be seen from the international space station where chimpanzees break records of human achievement. California is burning. Against our landlord's wishes you painted the bathroom plum. The Supreme Court ruled against the great elephant die off, their enormous gray ears unconstitutionally settling into shallow pools of mud. No one wore masks or even considered the possibility of dreamers. The winner of the election mounted the podium and flew away. According to sources all of Potosí is bracing for flight. General Motors is shutting down the museum of childhood artifacts. A once-in-a-century solar eclipse but I couldn't bring myself to go outside that day. The San Andreas fault line, along with the disappeared women, were a hoax. Someone whispered "choice" and a sinkhole opened up beneath them in Florida. The evidence corroborates but

The Bachelor just started. A hurricane sweeps over the Sierra Madres and tornado Adam bleaches coral in the gulf. In a small town in Colorado lovers protest in hunger strike. The earth is a triangle, and everything else a Mobius strip.

My Names

for Sandra Cisneros

It's like your vowels and consonants have run away from you, but not too far, they always come back. It's the sound of dirt loosening from fingernails, of a big world disintegrating beneath a steady stream. It's my father, whose favorite time of day is sunrise, or my mother, who always woke before him.

It was supposed to be Angela. That's what my mother wanted but she wanted a lot of things. And some of it she got, or came within spitting distance of, but more often than not she was silent. So many years later I wonder if my life would have been different, with this name. What kind of person would Angela be—would she be doubtful or calculating or chaste? Would she be a dreamer, leaning with her whole body into the swollen territory of sleep?

Angelica Maria. Seven syllables. Thirteen letters. Say it out loud. Pay attention to the way your mouth moves, how your tongue lunges up to the front teeth and back down again. It's what my father wanted. And my grandfather agreed, what a pretty name, so much better than Angela. I wonder how my mother's face looked, lying in the maternity ward, surrounded by the men in her life. I hope her features betrayed her thoughts, but I doubt it.

Seven Ways of Looking at Tayeko's Hands

    I
two juicy navels
ripened during fire season
the ash, the smoke, the aromatic fleshy chambers
distilled into russet chin glaze

    II
strips of county roadmaps dipped
in glue, wrapped around a wire hanger frame
let dry two hours, or three
throw away papier-mâché

    III
drop seeds into clay-laden soil
& sit on a severed tree stump looking up
indignant for rain
none comes
generations later an apartment complex sprouts
& the trim is the same muted color
you imagine your nationalism to be

    IV
one of three sons throws a football &—as is
written in the ancient prophecy—
glass breaks
tiptoeing around the carpet
you glance down and see hundreds of you
reflected back in the shards
insect eyes;
multitudinous—

        V
loom of merciful things woven
maker
tuck spools of stringy hair behind
deafened ears
sleep silently to rhythmic click of foot tapping
at machine

        VI
the Santa Anas whip through the
Valley of Discarded Childhood Toys
before dying out in the Canyon of
Subjective Truths
a past divined
from an ovoid stain on the linoleum
after a long day of porch gazing
you fold clothes into precise
cotton envelopes

        VII
your hands
calloused & obstinate
architectural anomalies
nothing you touch
falls victim to revision
you once quelled my tantrum
by placing a bird's nest
on my forehead

He Says My Country

Whereas the mustard flowers spread
       indiscriminately across the watershed

Whereas in realist oil paintings it is
       understood the sea extends

beyond the canvas edge.
       Let it not be conversational, or an

answer, or metaphor. No dreams wait
       in line holding forged documents. Whereas

the goodbye is cut short by a line of grievers
       exiting the parking lot in starched jeans.

Summoning Quetzals

We named you
before you were
a thing to be named.
We drummed the rhythm
of your heart
before it knew
blood;
laced your crib
with frankincense
& waiting.
Miniatures lined
the bookshelves like
materialized prayers to
Mother.
We dreamed you
and it gave us flight.
Our teeth fell backward
into our gums,
the wave reversed
course swelling deeper
into ocean's
core.
Dawn receding
could not scatter images
of
your face.
I abstain from future
wanting
should you let us
count you
among the messes
we've made.

DREAMS TOUCHING WATER

"To extract each fragment by each fragment from the word from the image another word another image the reply that will not repeat history in oblivion."

Theresa Hak Kyung Cha

Signs Foretelling the Fall of the Aztecs

A decontextualized lightning bolt,
unaccompanied by rumbling or rain,
ruptured the atmosphere to strike
a sacred site.

/

At another temple, fire.
They siphoned the aqueduct into
hollowed gourds,
drenched the heat with mountain water
but the flames did not relent.
Emboldened, its golden fingers
reached higher until they merged with
the underbelly of the sun.

/

Then there was the inconsolable wail
of a woman. Her melancholy
passed between houses in the dark,
invisibly,
so that whomever moved to pity her
found their arms wrapped around
a humid night.

/

There was even a bird—
prophecies so often winged.
Its smoky plumage human eyes had never before
beheld. It was captured &

presented to the
Mighty Motecuhzoma as he reclined
on the precipice of something
that had yet to be given a name.

Weren't all gods birds in one way
or another.
Motecuhzoma stirred from the apogee,
welcomed the feathered creature into his
square hands as his great-great-great-
grandmother had squeezed her palms together to collect
the first droplet of water to ever fall from
a darkened cloud.
Remarkable in its
singularity, the bird's forehead bore a silver disk,
a mirror,
on which a name sharpened into
the image of a foreigner's boat
docking on the eastern shore.

Motecuhzoma squinted.

The disk's theater shifted:
now, dying
in the plains,
the fine points of arrows
piercing tissue, organs,
everyone he knew crumpling to the ground.
Alarmed, the great prince called upon others to bear witness
to the bird's prophecy.
But when they gathered the image withdrew.

The bird, nestled benevolently between
Motecuhzoma's hands, slept.

/

Even the stars bore the mark of
impending blood. Violence steamed
up from the dirt, circulated lungs
to mix in the birthplace
of primordial
song.

//

But
what if
it wasn't written?
Malintzin Tenepal come back
& we will lay turquoise at your feet.
You will carry our last names
& your mouth will be full
of chocolate.
Forgive us our betrayal
we did not know our ignorance
weighed heavier than
the strength of
your wet tongue.

In Every Way the Wrong One

My father never read a book in his life

He said, you spend too much time worrying over something that
will never love you back

He came to the states when he was a boy and slept on his brother's
floor

It was before Orange County became an artery of Jalisco's longing

Before he fucked one too many putas and mom left him for a
financial aid specialist

Before the world touched him, the bottle and god

Before he naturalized, filed bankruptcy and stopped showing up
for custody hearings

Before he moved in with Tia Mago in Lake Elsinore where he
traded labor for rent

Pulling a lawn mower across the parched earth, sweating through
muscle tees

The sun bronzing the stripe of his neck

Songs sobbing from the radio propped on a plastic chair

I was in every way the wrong one

With my crop tops and name brand shoes, pretending I could only
hear English

My eyes brimmed with the families on TV gathering at the end of
    each episode to moralize their mistakes

And I thought: if I try hard enough I can will away the hair from
    my upper lip

I can read myself into the life of the fictitious girl who on page
    12 is described as a sunflower

Leaning into early autumn light

And now, so many years have shed from the lining of our hungers

He and his new woman in a trailer off the 15 highway

Pushing 20 dollars into my hand when I come visit from the university

These moments of atonement are their own kind of migration

Their own kind of sob, or dream or dismissal

Recently, we have taken to calling one another at night to make
    sense of the stars

Our Orphanhood We Live

what if i / opened my center
split out / purple mouthed & screaming
a child / who is also / a river

what if I became / rocks
& carried you / & cradled
re / forested visions

resume :: reeds
resume :: creaturely markings

these sodden / feel / ds

blinking-eye rainfall / would become /
you / becoming us /

we would always / be
dear river / deer
/ our breaths' rhythm /
paced / out
/ in swollen age

together /
unmaking / making
/ riding snow / melt
down / annals of antiquity
ever / soon / ever
/ ridgeline to estuary
 warp to weft

in / the practice / of
becoming / salt /

ALTAR:

photo: your mother as a teenager, standing in a field of tall flowers
    in Vietnam.

    Three amateur, vague shapes we whittled from wood—
    porcupine? Whale? Selena's ghost?

    Copal, mine.

    Bundled sage, yours.

photo: my grandmothers, Maria and Tayeko, in the late eighties.
    They do not speak the same

    language yet their arms conspiratorially link as they sit on
    the couch and gaze at the camera, unsmiling.

    Virgen de Guadalupe candle, mine.

    Tupac candle, yours.

photo: your childhood brown husky, appropriately named Brownie.

photo: your childhood black husky, inappropriately named Blackie.

photo: my great grandfather whom I never met. He lived to be 104.

    Cow figurine, yours.

    Prayer flags, yours.

    Dried flowers from Trader Joes, mine.

photo: your handsome Uncle Seven looking pensive, a fading jungle
    crowding the background of the shot. He wears a pressed
    white shirt with sleeves rolled halfway up his bronze arms.

    Incense with holder, ours.

    Money effigies, yours.

    Lava rock, quartzite and a shell from San Onofre, mine.

    Bite-sized Buddhist teachings from the temple printed on
    small pieces of blue paper, yours.

    Box of matches, mine.

photo: Tayeko in sepia tones, taken off guard by the photographer,
    wearing dark lipstick. It was likely taken in Long Beach
    shortly before she met my grandfather. She looks luminous.

Rainbow

And when the clouds parted a fat rainbow arched across the shifting sky, perfectly framing the Stater Brothers parking lot, freeway onramp, Holy Grail Thrift. Briefly, Wonder released its tendrils into the city. The light turned red and I slowed to a stop. I reached over the center console to grab your shoulder. *Look! It's a rainbow!* I gasped. It was maybe too sentimental for you but I pleaded. *Look baby. Just look. It's so beautiful. Can't you just turn your head and*—green again, so I drove onward. Your gaze remained on your phone screen, and then it just disappeared.

Your Last Day, a Hammer

For Vanessa Guillen

                looking

        into yr

                newspaper photograph

    I see

the grainy filaments of a sunday
                                morning
        three egg yolks
leftover wine

yr face:

                you look like you could be my sister

        a mestiza
with a wide Iberian nose
        full bottom lip that cracks the mouth open

laughter shooting through gap teeth

yr skin

        a shade

                darker

                        than my family would've liked

                    at communions

          you'd be fussed over

          with a tube

     of sunscreen
               directed to sit

                              under
                    piecemeal

                                        shad
                                        e—

     you could've been

               my

          lay-beneath-a-tree-trunk-to-study-the-habits-of-flocking-crows

          my

               daydream

          manifesto

first

     experience

          of

          color

               my

                if-we're-both-not-married-by-the-time-we're-46

the person with whom

I combine
        tools

                as the sky

        pulses
    orange

            then gray

        above
    Us

the last
                letter

                        I write before

            the last
        tree

            in the last
        forest

        splits

                is addressed to you:

        the person to whom I gift a sour
        peach

      and later

a lock of oil

    black hair

            the final person I thank

    as I accept an award on behalf of

streaming women

      my

      my

     but who am I

       to claim you?

           I discard

        the news like

            peeled

              skin

Rapture, Tonka Trucks & Tea Parties

A man loiters in the Walmart parking lot with a shopping cart full of puppies. I approach with caution; you rush over and with rare abandon lean yr face into the furry mass and coo. Pup cradled to chest, you look over at me for permission. No. Not now, with a second story apartment abutting the freeway. Not with a nosy landlord who, in response to the potted jungle of clippings taken from neighbors' yards, limited the amount of outdoor plants that could line our porch to four. Not with the overturned coffee table in the living room.

Against my better judgment the puppy sits in our kitchen looking up at me. Blinking with one big blue eye the color of cold water and one big brown eye the same color as my own. I go to brush my teeth and he follows. He pees on the floor of the bathroom while I pee sitting on the toilet. I build a barricade out of books and boxes and put him on one side while I sit on the other. The distance I've created confuses him. He whines, then yawns, eventually nodding off to sleep with one paw tucked beneath his chin, the other vaguely reaching in my direction. I quietly stand and go work in the adjacent room. Within seconds, he yelps. The yelps escalate to wails. The wails into screams. The desperation is acute—like he's being skinned alive, like he's being submerged into a giant vat of hot swirling oil—and it only ceases once I re-enter his line of sight. At which point he dozes off again. You come home late. I don't remember if you kiss my forehead before or after loosening yr tie. I ask you a question about yr day and it goes unanswered. I ask again and still no response. But of course, yr already asleep, laying on top of the covers with phone resting gently in hand.

And then, despite the growing list of things that need my attention, it's time for shots. I close my laptop, switch over the laundry, and load the pup into the backseat of the car. The man in the Walmart parking lot had said the pup was a boy but the vet confirms otherwise. *He* is actually a *she*. A girl. Hard to tell at first because of the unusual size of her anatomy. I think: our puppy has a big vulva. A big confusing disproportionate vulva. On the drive home I don't understand the stinging in my eyes. I never cry. It's just simply not the way I express my emotions, not my particular brand of breaking apart before gathering together and trudging onward. Tears converge and slip off my jaw like rain down a window. I glance at her in the back seat and am seized by a feeling. Halfway home I recognize it: rapture. In every other aspect of my life I eschew the constructs of gender. I rally against bratz dolls and football and Tonka Trucks and princess plots. I pair hot shorts with hairy legs, a buzzed head with blush. Except now. The pup is a girl. A little girl. And she's reaching her wet nose across the center console into my awaiting hand.

WHAT WE WEREN'T TAUGHT

A poem about a hanging tree but missing
the ineluctable sensory implosion
       of
       seeinghearingsmellingflyingshudderingpullingawaybrawling-
       disembowlingsquishingaccostingpiercingpleadingrepuls-
       ingthrobbing

as the fleshy neck
splits

Somewhere a poem about a hanging tree pays homage
to the landscaper who last pruned it
or the bird who shit the seed last millenia while flying across El Paso
on its way to some other apocalypse

"Too many poems about hanging trees"

             —says tree cut down for pulp
             —says history professor as he squints his
             eyes in the reflection of a porcelain urinal

human footprints found
in New Mexico
carbon dated
23,000 years
old

     "proof"

of what the sandstone always
already knew

what— when the planet
        orbits without us —
        it will hold in its
        memory

        what we now hold in our
                dry hands:

   history / foiled /

ziggurats to detention centers
serpents to mules

mythos of grass
to object of archeological study

     hewn
        fragments
   piece
together
     a
       crisis

     unutterable

the past a thirst
scarring our throats
from the constancy
    of wanting

That Fool

I become monstrous

the things he did

retaliates

only a believer's

could translate

I've been called

to keep it

keep it

this [body part] here

I hold

a cavern

countless tiny grains

to trace

or blame

speaking aloud

my mouth

turns to dust

cry

the vocabulary

on to adopt

textbook

neutral—

that [body part]

in my hands

of sand

too insignificant

or count

High Desert Couplets

A mustache far rivaling
Emilio's, turned cloud-wise.

Drying on their descent
to pile at her boots.

Between us, an invisible
assembly of strings.

I lean down to her lips
& am startled by the brush.

Loosening into unintelligible
matter, becoming green.

In the cabinet a family recipe
for quail with rose petal sauce.

Your spine a poetry of knots
I read with deft fingers.

How to know you're dreaming
When you're dreaming, lesson one.

As the tornado of dust curtsied
at the edge of the property line.

Now, she said, as if it were an answer
to a question.

On Nights I Weep Chocolate

Our indigenous & african blood
you kept from me
hallucinating a s t r a i g h t l i n e
tracing our last name

back

to a well-documented
new / world / bound
ship.

We are forty-seventh-sixteen-zero-twelvth
generation—
I was told, playing cowboys
with the cousins
—castillian.
Undiluted;
our skin unimpeachable, look
at who we aren't,
over there,
in the graves.

It wasn't until
years later trying to conceive
a child, undergoing
genetic testing that I
uncovered: our whiteness is a lie.

& now it's all I see in y/our
forehead,
in y/our wide feet & tired eyes.

Our blood is a pillage
of a hemisphere,
orbiting an ambivalent universe
upside down.

Women's Clinic, Riverside 10:47 AM

a hysteroscopy in translation

The microscope pushes through fleshy insides. I tilt my gaze to witness the procedure on screen: my uterus a grainy film without sound. The director a doctor who, with the right insurance, auditions women for the coveted role of childbearing. A light emanates from the tip of the microscope illuminating what would otherwise be dark, light. Dusty rose catacombs sharpen into focus. Chiaroscuro veins pulsate. It's a silent film. In language's place a score—the music of my knees as they bend against the stirrups.

All for the so-called "money shot." Today it's a visual scan of the polyp and—if we're lucky, doctor says—a sample of the errant tissue. She maneuvers the camera left, upward, deeper inside. The instrument scrapes. My womb relents. A collection, she calls it, like it's numerous. Blood tendrils crowd the camera lens, helixing and collapsing at half speed. I too hold my breath. Avert my eyes. I don't, at first, recognize it as a wound. And when I do it becomes all too familiar. Cue montage: a steady stream of mild intrusions. Me growing up in an apartment under red water. The exhaustion of it. Cue return to present day: I squeeze your hand. You don't understand that I want you to squeeze back.

Doctor retracts the glimmering sample, emerging from my sex to enclose it in a pre-labeled vial. There is triumph in the way her eyes meet mine. The camera blurs then goes black. The screen clicks off. You launch into an animated description of something inconsequential. It's not until later I realize it's to distract me from the blood. It pools beneath the table. As I stand it clumps down my thighs, staining the linoleum and my bare feet. I'm not a stranger to this excess but the context is all wrong. An assistant appears to clean me, embarrassed by her task. I want to take the towels from her: I have my own rituals, my own patterns for removing parts of me that are no longer tucked inside. I've mastered this pulling together. I can walk out of this office like I've walked out of dark hallways and subsidized housing with beer cans erupting from the trash. Like my very existence depended on being slack-jawed, eyes unfocused, brows unclenched; my entire face a conspiracy of indifference, mutely accepting the sequence of events that somehow must accumulate into a day.

GLOSSARY OF COMMON SYMBOLS

In the dream, I am always met at the river

Cherríe Moraga

Last Winter, a Dialectic

The sperm arrived the night I learned Abuelita Maria was on her deathbed.

It came encased in a nitrogen tank, in a giant yellow industrial chest. The straw itself, dwarfed by the packaging, was tiny. The size of a chance: anemic and fragile.

The month before Maria had celebrated her 94th birthday with an ice cream cake and mariachi. She beamed, danced, and sent eye daggers to my stepmom as she poured my father another drink. Grandchildren and great grandchildren slipped in and out of view. The moon cast muted silver shadows across the plastic tables, her cheeks.

As the party endured its final song, dawn cresting the foothills of the Sierra Madres, Maria tugged on my father's sleeve. She pulled him closer. He was her not-so-secret favorite of eight children, and she chided him for working too much. She noted his back was growing hunched, his spine compressed after decades of gravity and sweat.

She used to complain to me about aging. She'd grab the excess skin on her forearms and tug. *See*, she'd implore. *Look at this. Look how ugly I've become.* I was a child. I had no frame of reference, no true or studied conception of time; I could intellectually grasp that one day I'd be old like Abuelita, but I couldn't yet internalize it in my body, feel or know it in any meaningful measure. I never knew how to respond to her lamentations. I listened and, when she abated, offered her coffee.

The instructions recommended the use of gloves for removing the specimen from the tank. It also suggested cross referencing the specimen number on the straw with the invoice to ensure we received the correct donor's sperm. This you did, in the precise way you approach anything involving numbers and documents. Sliding your slim fingers through white rubber, snapping the gloves taut to your wrists.

While the specimen thawed on the nightstand you ran tentative fingers through my hair. *Ten minutes*, you said, starting a timer. You untied my robe and kissed my darkening nipples.

Now that I'm older I realize I should have picked her a bouquet of backyard grasses. Or gently held her wrists.

Abuelita Maria's health rapidly deteriorated over the course of several long, somber days. All of her surviving children returned to Talpa to be with her, so soon after the birthday trip, their suitcases not fully unpacked before they were refitted with black. There was no dancing or chiding. She stopped taking food, then water. She inhaled a final shaky breath and never released it.

My dad called to relay the news. *She's gone*, he said. *She's gone she's gone*. For a moment I thought he might cry but instead he cleared his throat. He said the funeral is going to be small because of

COVID so I should just stay home. I needn't bother making the trip. Someone yelled to him from another room, and then he hung up.

We thought, hands on my belly, that maybe this was the price. A life for a life. We never spoke it aloud but we felt justified asking for a child. We felt like the scales were tipped in our favor, like we deserved at least one good thing. All night we mourned and prayed to nothing in particular, because we were both nonbelievers, only vaguely invested in our respective cultures' mythos of fate, the universe—its gifts and exactments.

After the funeral I called my dad and asked if he could locate a painting. So many years ago—a lifetime, really—when my parents were still together, Abuelita Maria came to the states and met my maternal grandmother, Tayeko.

Tayeko was an artist, a painter, and she gifted Maria a portrait she'd made. It was of a young, pious looking girl cloaked in blue and gazing beyond the edge of the canvas at some-

thing arresting, maybe mirac-
ulous. Maria accepted the gift.
She assessed it. Pleased, she
nodded. She carried it back
to her country wrapped in
towels, tape.

We woke with our hands clasped
together every morning that
followed, so sanguine we were
at the possibility of our baby.
We hoped and then tried not
to hope too much. We warned
each other against it, citing
things like odds and statistics,
chance and cycle fluctuations,
attempting to stem future disap-
pointment. So we masked our
hope and kept it close. We
held it to ourselves, willfully
ignoring the electricity in the
air and the sweet sweet promise
of spring rain.

Once my dad returned to the
states I went over to his place
and there it was, the painting
that tied my grandmothers
together across lifetimes and
nations, propped against an arm
of the couch. The ornate frame
was chipped around the corners.
Yet the girl's face remained
pious. The years never touched
her the way they touched and
remade us. My dad said he was

happy I asked for it, because I was the only person left for whom it meant anything.

And then I felt it. First as a pang in my abdomen, then as a reluctant wetness between my thighs. Okay, I thought. Well.

The afternoon came and went. Your face, for only the briefest of moments, slipped when you came home and found me, feet wedged into the toilet seat, squatting over the bowl.

Next month. We'll try again next month, you said, with such certainty that I believed it to be fact. I met your eyes and nodded as beneath me hope slipped wild and red into the water, darkening irrevocably everything it touched.

I Hope the Water Remembers Me Because I Remember the Water

water

cold water

blue green water

water song

algae water bodies

watercolor prophet

globular water sky

    water weep

    water sob

    tepid water eroding

    glacial water cutting

    bracken water occluding the swollen corpses of teachers

    waterlogged, sopping, snaked around an idea

    of sunkissed water pools

    water boxed and bottled

    water seams streaming through urban sanctuaries

    through constellations heavy with satellite debris

a fool's water

a fortune's water

a lie to bring the water back

saturated roots of cactus water

water cresting, weaving and falling

clouds giving themselves over

losing themselves in water swoons

    purple water veins

    arterial water pumping the heart

    manuscripts soaked in water longing

    water girls

    turned water bois

    the true cost of water

glowing vessels of fire water, a comet, a comment

origami water folding into cranes

batting wings to ease into water landing

water to wash away factory grit

water to wash away theories of water

water to wash away iridescent swirls of oil

helixing clockwise on watery slopes

where water is mythic

tall tale water with eyes the size of carp

snowballing with atmospheric dust

water welt

water ache

apparitions of ghost water

haunting crevasses on the moon

reaching from the water's deep

life water

life

Eʟ Nɪño 1994, 2019

Wind whips through the tenements,
 and it rains.
  The pilot of the stove refuses to light,
   and it rains
    Younger versions of ourselves spray paint
     benign propaganda
      in streaks of opal and blue,
       and it rains.

       The sky wrings itself in a rhythm
        close to texting.

        On tv, a worm drowns
         in a field of poppies.

         My memory is weather.
         The horizon opens up
          to a theater of wanting:

            I dance for you,
             back hunched in the shape of a whale,
            to a flood song
             long abandoned.

          Soon the clouds will break
           into a million undefined pieces.
          Moths will scatter
           from porch lights and we will be unrecognizable
          in a rippling surface.
          Everything will be drenched
           and clinging.

Indelible In The Hippocampus Is The Laughter

When yr a fourteen year old girl yr body is a public   men's gazes loiter near the
bathrooms or anytime you walk down the street even   in yr own
neighborhood even in the neighborhood of yr cousin or anytime   you walk
down any street in any city in any lush or barren geography   the atmosphere
pressing upon yr skin like a too heavy hand every day is a dream   sequence
everyone's dream face altered to reveal their barest thirst   their eyes endless
black pits that track you as you walk from yr locker to class   yr locker to the
parking lot yr locker as the nexus from which all yr   movements orchestrate
even when you come home the eyes will be on you as you   change into sweatpants
they will step onto the air conditioning unit to glimpse you   while you shower
& when you catch them they will laugh & their laughter   will cling as the
understanding dawns that there is no waking up   there is only growing
older yet the laughter never ages   it'll be just as crisp & sharp as when
you were first learning how to shave   yr legs because the hair it grew overnight &
it grew with a vengeance &   next came the talons within weeks feathers
appeared how they sprouted   like weeds along the dips of yr spine a blue so dark
it took all the light with it   & then yr voice broke & in its place resounded an
uncertain maw & this is the secret voice   of all women & when the black
eyes follow & leer & undress   you &   when the sticky fingers follow suit & yr
skin & hair & feathers & talons   & the whole fucking goddam world are stained
with the grease of lust that isn't   yrs you'll feel like a monster & you swear that
no one would ever want to touch   yr body if they knew what a disaster it
was this is the truth of it   the truth of dreaming & waking & being &
wanting & knowing   they just keep grabbing the disaster & pushing the
disaster into the dark   & naming the disaster a cunt & following the disaster on
foot & you   walk briskly & keep yr claws retracted & refuse to turn when
they   speak yr name as if it belongs to them as if they invented you & yr
monstrosity   which they mistake as beauty their crowning achievement their
basest life's work

Barbed Wire Motif

how many
times does the
river
start
and stop
in yr mouth

We did
not dream
equally

Sweet grasses
grow
like a soft
pelt over
yr secret
face

MIDLIFE PASTORAL

When to stop, I said
aloud, while walking
the dog.
She paused to smell the base
of a palm tree.
She peed on it:

"I am here."

And I suppose so were we,
holding the leash,
respectfully
averting our gazes
as she finished up and scratched
the surrounding
grass.

Some people
tease
that couples start
to look alike
as they age
together, as years fall
away like petals
from a picked flower.
    Dogs too.

I couldn't help
but think that to others
the trio of us

are a single image,
a contained
synonymous
stream
of colors and lines.
And maybe to others
we are made
whole
in our resemblance
as if One
were an ultimate state
any addition could
compromise.

A squirrel skittered
across the road
and the dog whimpered
to be let
free.

We like to think of ourselves
as the kind of people
who would unclasp
the leash
but
a bicyclist rode by
and we couldn't
trust that she'd return
to us after understanding
the squirrel
would never be
caught.

A Somnambulist's Guide to Morning

In dreams I stir to prowl the house, the vegetable
garden, in search of your stray touch. I bound and trouble.
The moon lowers, the orange sun rises. Solitude stretches across
the horizon in a dreary yawn. Defeated, I track my muddy feet

through the kitchen, down the hallway lined with
photos of other people's children. I return to bed and reach,
and somehow there you are, memory made bone,
a forgotten constant, self-contained beneath the covers.

Peaceful—
your face eases into Mythic past. *As if* the war never scorched
the island, the boat fare remained untendered, bobbing
forever at Vung Tau delivered from the depths
of an uncertain night; *as if* the crash reversed course
and your mother's life hadn't been taken that unspeakable day so
many long years gone.

In sleep, your face mirrors the easy confidence
of the forest. I roll into your warmth, breathe in your familiar
musk, and allay into the mercy of abstract dreams. Time resumes.
We wake, together, as dawn saturates the room. Our bodies
humid where they press. And we gaze up at the ceiling as if
it wasn't a ceiling at all but our own personal sky everlasting.

Eden Redux

i regret not coming over for christmas
i know i'm a heathen in the blue eyes of god
i sin & i sin again & revel in the sticky
sweetness of my lover's trans body i roll
& smoke too much grass with my feet propped
on the porch's busted railing i swear & laugh too loudly
with too much of my belly in a giggle fit i'll stain my pants
yellow slap my knee like i'm trying to wake it from death
like i'm my own imaginary friend

the orange jumpsuit I was issued in county
made me feel like I was in a TLC music video i'm so
proudly divorced it was one of the best decisions
i've made to date i pray for moonlight & fermentation
i touch myself to sci-fi smut & to mushroom induced
fantasies of what else is possible i stroke strangers
to revolutionary podcasts or on quieter nights
to the sound of amy goodman as she parleys
the world's tragedies on donation-based tv

i regret not going home because i know
you'd welcome me anyway fix me a plate
with the three tamales of three hundred that you didn't
stuff with meat just for me you've never asked me
to apologize or raised a brow at my sex stained
neck in fact i even overheard you giggling with Tia Rosa
if you were born today in the states like me
you would've stayed out all night & returned home
smelling like eve as she locked gazes with adam
& guided the apple to her teeth

The Daughter After Me

        Will grow to be the Good One. She's expected to
answer in Spanish—
and she does, flawlessly, while arranging toy kitchen utensils
    on the carpet.

Massacre of Dreamers

*It's nearing midnight and something holy is always coming around. Take
love for instance, and the bare perfect neck of a woman who's given up every-
thing for the forbidden leap —Joy Harjo*

& who among us
will be the next Zapata?

Will it be Eli with his
sloppy line-end rhyme,

or Chuy, in all his
next generation glory?

I think the revolution
will be a womxn,

with skin as dark as oil
& jeans too tight for pockets.

Come night she'll sneak
into my bedroom

& undress me piece by piece
until there's nothing left

but my hope inside her fists.
She'll be a gentle lover.

She'll remember all my favorite fruits
& never forget to set the alarm.

Over a pot of coffee she'll ask
to braid my hair. I slide between her

legs onto the cool kitchen tile,
her knees bracketing my neck

& I admit: I've loved more causes
than have loved me

I've slept with more ideas
than with anything that breathes

That sometimes I feel too old, too
young, too tired to ask questions.

To which she replies: comrade,
luchadora, enamorada, mijita,

es tiempo para levantarnos.
With her, my words are never rendered

too small. & when she leaves
it's while I'm sleeping.

The revolution escapes
until morning, leaving behind

a sense of urgency, a warmth
between my sheets too steady

to cool with my own quavering self doubt,
& a pistola on the nightstand,

thick with our sweaty fingerprints,
barrel aiming toward the open window.

About the Author

Angelica Maria Barraza Tran is a writer / teacher / lover / avid wanderer / cloud enthusiast. She lives in California with her partner and animal pack.

About The Hillary Gravendyk Prize

The Hillary Gravendyk Prize is an open poetry book competition published by Inlandia Institute for all writers regardless of the number of previously published poetry collections.

HILLARY GRAVENDYK (1979-2014) was a beloved poet living and teaching in Southern California's "Inland Empire" region. She wrote the acclaimed poetry book, *HARM* from Omnidawn Publishing (2012) and the posthumoussly published *The Soluble Hour* (Omnidawn, 2017) and *Unlikely Conditions* (1913 Press, 2017, with Cynthia Arrieu-King) as well as the poetry chapbook *The Naturalist* (Anchiote Press, 2008). A native of Washington State, she was an admired Assistant Professor of English at Pomona College in Claremont, CA. Her poetry has appeared widely in journals such as *American Letters & Commentary*, *The Bellingham Review*, *The Colorado Review*, *The Eleventh Muse*, *Fourteen Hills*, *MARY*, *1913: A Journal of Forms*, *Octopus Magazine*, *Tarpaulin Sky* and *Sugar House Review*. She was awarded a 2015 Pushcart Prize for her poem "Your Ghost," which appeared in the Pushcart Prize Anthology. She leaves behind many devoted colleagues, friends, family and beautiful poems. Hillary Gravendyk passed away on May 10, 2014 after a long illness. This contest has been established in her memory.

About Inlandia Institute

Inlandia Institute is a regional non-profit and literary center. We seek to bring focus to the richness of the literary enterprise that has existed in this region for ages. The mission of the Inlandia Institute is to recognize, support, and expand literary activity in all of its forms in Inland Southern California by publishing books and sponsoring programs that deepen people's awareness, understanding, and appreciation of this unique, complex and creatively vibrant region.

The Institute publishes books, presents free public literary and cultural programming, provides in-school and after school enrichment programs for children and youth, holds free creative writing workshops for teens and adults, and boot camp intensives. In addition, every two years, the Inlandia Institute appoints a distinguished jury panel from outside of the region to name an Inlandia Literary Laureate who serves as an ambassador for the Inlandia Institute, promoting literature, creative literacy, and community. Laureates to date include Susan Straight (2010-2012), Gayle Brandeis (2012-2014), Juan Delgado (2014-2016), Nikia Chaney (2016-2018), and Rachelle Cruz (2018-2020).

To learn more about the Inlandia Institute, please visit our website at www.InlandiaInstitute.org.

Other Hillary Gravendyk Prize Books

Our Lady of Perpetual Desert by Alexandra Martinez
Winner of the 2021 Regional Hillary Gravendyk Prize

among the enemies by Michael Samra
Winner of the 2020 National Hillary Gravendyk Prize

This Side of the Fire by Jonathan Maule
Winner of the 2020 Regional Hillary Gravendyk Prize

The Silk the Moths Ignore by Bronwen Tate
Winner of the 2019 National Hillary Gravendyk Prize

Remyth: A Postmodern Ritual by Adam D. Martinez
Winner of the 2019 Regional Hillary Gravendyk Prize

All the Emergency-Type Structures by Elizabeth Cantwell
Winner of the 2018 Regional Hillary Gravendyk Prize

Our Bruises Kept Singing Purple by Malcolm Friend
Winner of the 2017 National Hillary Gravendyk Prize

Traces of a Fifth Column by Marco Maisto
Winner of the 2016 National Hillary Gravendyk Prize

God's Will for Monsters by Rachelle Cruz
Winner of the 2016 Regional Hillary Gravendyk Prize
Winner of a 2018 American Book Award

Map of an Onion by Kenji C. Liu
Winner of the 2015 National Hillary Gravendyk Prize

All Things Lose Thousands of Times by Angela Peñaredondo
Winner of the 2015 Regional Hillary Gravendyk Prize